THE BUCK STOPS HERE

THE BUCK STOPS HERE
WORDS OF WISDOM
FROM THE DESKS
OF 77 SUCCESSFUL PEOPLE

HORACE MARTIN WOODHOUSE

COPYRIGHT NOTICE

THE BUCK STOPS HERE: Words of Wisdom from the Desks of 77 Successful People is published and copyrighted © 2009, by History Company (www.historycompany.com). All rights reserved. No part of this book may be reproduced in any form by any electronic or mechanical means (including photocopying, recording, or information storage or retrieval) without permission in writing from the publisher. Users are not permitted to mount any part of this book on the World Wide Web.

Direct-from-Publisher discounts are available for educators wanting to use our books in the classroom, and for charitable organizations wishing to sell History Company books for fundraisers.

For more information, send email to: support@historycompany.com

ISBN: 978-0-9787368-5-9

Printed in the United States of America.

SIGNS OF SUCCESS

You can tell something about a man by what he keeps on his desk, and you can tell something about a woman by what she keeps on her desk. Sayings and quotes that people place on a desktop or post on an office wall often represent a personal credo, a statement of values, a guiding principle they intend to follow on a path to success.

By placing the sign "The Buck Stops Here" on his desk, President Truman was stating categorically that he was responsible for all decisions made in the Oval Office. It was his constant reminder that no one else would take the blame for the way the country was governed. Just as his desk sign came to express Truman's decisiveness and accountability, we have found many other examples, 77 to be exact, in which successful people have used words of wisdom as daily inspiration.

The desk signs and office wall mottos on the following pages offer reminders of the importance of individual vision and commitment as they display values, purpose and beliefs, aspirations and philosophy. It's a fascinating view into social, economic and political history, as well as the individual influences on a remarkable group of accomplished men and women. We hope you will enjoy discovering the secrets of their success.

Henry Ford

Founder of the Ford Motor Company and father of modern assembly lines used in mass production, Henry Ford's introduction of the Model T automobile heralded the beginning of the Motor Age; the car evolved from luxury item for the well-to-do to essential transportation for the ordinary man.

As owner of the Ford Company he became one of the richest and best-known people in the world. Ford had a global vision, with consumerism as the key to peace. Ford did not believe in accountants; he amassed one of the world's largest fortunes without ever having his company audited under his administration.

Henry Ford's intense commitment to lowering costs resulted in many technical and business innovations, including a franchise system that put a dealership in every city in North America, and in major cities on six continents.

THINK YOU CAN.
THINK YOU CAN'T.
EITHER WAY, YOU'RE RIGHT.

ALBERT EINSTEIN

He was the German-born theoretical physicist, best known for his theory of relativity and specifically mass-energy equivalence, expressed by the equation $E = mc^2$. He received the 1921 Nobel Prize in Physics.

Einstein's other contributions to physics include advances in the fields of relativistic cosmology, capillary action, critical opalescence, classical problems of statistical mechanics and their application to quantum theory, an explanation of the Brownian movement of molecules, atomic transition probabilities, the quantum theory of a monatomic gas, thermal properties of light with low radiation density (which laid the foundation for the photon theory), a theory of radiation including stimulated emission, the conception of a unified field theory, and the geometrization of physics.

When asked where he got his scientific ideas, Einstein explained that he believed scientific work best proceeds from an examination of physical reality and a search for underlying axioms, with consistent explanations that apply in all instances and avoid contradicting each other.

> NOT EVERYTHING THAT COUNTS CAN BE COUNTED, AND NOT EVERYTHING THAT CAN BE COUNTED COUNTS.

TED TURNER

He has had a remarkable and visionary career, best known as founder of the cable television network CNN, the first dedicated 24-hour cable news channel.

Turner's media empire began with his father's billboard business, worth $1 million when he took it over in 1963. Long a philanthropist with deep pockets, he pledged a $1 billion gift to the United Nations in 1997; his is believed to be the largest donation by a single private individual in history.

He turned the Atlanta Braves baseball team into a nationally popular franchise and launched the charitable Goodwill Games. A lifelong sailing enthusiast, his boat Courageous won the 1977 America's Cup. In 1986 he purchased MGM Entertainment Company, including United Artists (MGM/UA), from Kirk Kerkorian, acquiring 3,650 motion pictures, including popular classics such as *Gone with the Wind*, *Citizen Kane* (Turner's favorite), and *Casablanca*. An interest in bison led Turner to establish Ted's Montana Grill, a chain of bison meat restaurants, in 2003.

LEAD, FOLLOW, OR GET OUT OF THE WAY.

Ronald Reagan

He was the 33rd Governor of California and 40th President of the United States. As president he pursued policies that reflected his personal belief in individual freedom, brought changes domestically, both to the U.S. economy and expanded military, and contributed to the end of the Cold War.

Reagan believed that if he could persuade the Soviets to allow for more democracy and free speech, this would lead to reform and the end of Communism.

Speaking at the Berlin Wall, on June 12, 1987, Reagan challenged Gorbachev to go further: "General Secretary Gorbachev, if you seek peace, if you seek prosperity for the Soviet Union and Eastern Europe, if you seek liberalization, come here to this gate! Mr. Gorbachev, open this gate! Mr. Gorbachev, tear down this wall."

> IT CAN BE DONE.

Rudolph Giuliani

Lawyer, prosecutor, businessman, and politician, Giuliani served two terms as Mayor of New York City, and was credited with initiating improvements in the city's quality of life and with a dramatic reduction in crime.

His period as mayor also saw allegations of civil rights abuses and other police misconduct. There were police shootings of unarmed suspects, and the scandals surrounding the sexual torture of Abner Louima and the killings of Amadou Diallo and Patrick Dorismond. However, Giuliani gained international attention during and after the September 11, 2001 attacks on the World Trade Center. In 2001, *Time* magazine named him "Person of the Year" and he received an honorary knighthood from Queen Elizabeth II.

I'M RESPONSIBLE.

PAUL NEWMAN

Seven-time Academy Award-nominated actor, Newman was also a film director, entrepreneur, humanitarian and auto racing enthusiast.

He won numerous awards, including an Academy Award for his performance in the 1986 Martin Scorsese film *The Color of Money*, three Golden Globe Awards, a BAFTA Award, a Screen Actors Guild Award, a Cannes Film Festival Award, an Emmy award, and many honorary awards. He also won several national championships as a driver in Sports Car Club of America road racing, and his race teams won several championships in open wheel IndyCar racing.

Newman was a co-founder of Newman's Own, a food company from which Newman donated all post-tax profits and royalties to charity.

> IF WE EVER HAVE A PLAN, WE'RE SCREWED.

DWIGHT D. EISENHOWER

Nicknamed "Ike," Dwight Eisenhower was a five-star general in the United States Army who served as Supreme Commander of the Allied forces in Europe, with responsibility for planning and supervising the successful invasion of France and Germany.

As President, he oversaw the cease-fire of the Korean War, kept up the pressure on the Soviet Union during the Cold War, made nuclear weapons a higher defense priority, launched the Space Race, enlarged the Social Security program, and began the Interstate Highway System.

In his farewell speech, Eisenhower warned us: "In the councils of government, we must guard against the acquisition of unwarranted influence, whether sought or unsought, by the military-industrial complex."

> # SUAVITER IN MODO, FORTITER IN RE.

(Gentle in manner, resolute in action)

JOHN F. KENNEDY

He was the thirty-fifth President of the United States, serving from 1961 until his assassination in 1963. As President, he set out to redeem his campaign pledge to get America moving again. His economic programs launched the country on its longest sustained expansion since World War II; before his death, he laid plans for a massive assault on persisting pockets of privation and poverty.

Admiral Rickover, who oversaw the development of the nation's nuclear navy and was the driving force behind the construction of the first nuclear-powered submarine, gave Kennedy this plaque inscribed with the Breton "Fisherman's Prayer" which the president kept on his desk in the Oval Office (the original plaque is on display in the Museum at the John F. Kennedy Library in Boston.

Brittany occupies a large peninsula in the northwest of France, lying between the English Channel to the north and the Bay of Biscay to the south. The region's livelihood has forever been intertwined with a sometimes unforgiving sea, and fishermen of Brittany utter a simple prayer when they launch their boats upon the deep.

> O GOD, THE SEA IS SO GREAT AND MY BOAT IS SO SMALL.

ROSS PEROT

He is an American businessman from Texas, who is best known for seeking the office of President of the United States in 1992 and 1996.

After he left the Navy in 1957, Perot became a salesman for International Business Machines (IBM). He quickly became a top employee, filling his year's sales quota in two weeks, and tried to pitch his ideas to supervisors who largely ignored him. He left IBM in 1962 to found Electronic Data Systems to computerize Medicare records. EDS went public in 1968 and the stock price shot up from $16 a share to $160 within days.

Fortune Magazine called Perot the "fastest, richest Texan" in a 1968 cover story. In 1984, General Motors bought EDS for $2.4 billion.

> EAGLES DON'T FLOCK.
> YOU HAVE TO FIND THEM
> ONE BY ONE.

JOSEPH J. JACOBS

In 1947 Joseph J. Jacobs went into business as Jacobs Engineering Company, operating as both an engineering consultant and a manufacturers' representative for process equipment.

When he retired, things started to go wrong under the new chief executive officer, and personnel relations also deteriorated badly. By the time he was persuaded to return, after about four years, bankruptcy was near at hand. He had two choices: accept bankruptcy or swim as strongly as he could for solid land far ahead.

Today the company is one of the world's largest and most diverse providers of professional technical services with annual revenues exceeding $11 billion.

BABE RUTH STRUCK OUT 1330 TIMES.

LOUIS V. GERSTNER

He was CEO of RJR Nabisco, and also held senior positions at American Express, where he spearheaded the successful "membership has its privileges" promotion, and at IBM, where he helped prevent the company from going out of business in the early 1990s.

He is a graduate of Chaminade High School, Dartmouth College and holds an MBA from Harvard Business School. In January, 2003, he assumed the position of chairman of The Carlyle Group, a global private equity firm located in Washington, DC. He retired from that position in October 2008 and remains a senior advisor to The Carlyle Group.

The quotation on his desk sign is from a novel by John le Carré, a favorite author.

> A DESK IS A DANGEROUS
> PLACE FROM WHICH
> TO VIEW THE WORLD.

SAM BROWNBACK

The senior United States Senator from the State of Kansas, Brownback is a leading social and fiscal conservative in Congress and an advocate for a smaller and compassionate government.

During 2007, he was a candidate in the Republican primaries for the 2008 Presidential election. He served as a White House Fellow in the first Bush Administration and was the youngest Secretary of Agriculture in Kansas history. Raised as a Methodist, Brownback later joined a nondenominational evangelical church, Topeka Bible Church, which he still regularly attends, even though in 2002, he converted to Catholicism.

The Second Commandment, inscribed on his desk plaque, is a guide to his political activism.

> LOVE YOUR NEIGHBOR AS YOURSELF.

KAREN KATEN

A senior executive at Pfizer, Karen Katen is one of the country's most highly respected business people.

She has worked for the international healthcare company since 1974 and has consistently been involved with the marketing of new products, including Viagra, which combats impotence, and Lipitor, which helps lower cholesterol. Her extraordinary success in introducing new medications to the American public has earned her many awards, as well as a ranking as one of America's fifty most powerful businesswomen.

In addition to serving as president of U.S. Pharmaceuticals Pfizer Incorporated, Katen holds several other influential posts at the company.

WHO ELSE NEEDS TO KNOW?

KAREN HUGHES

She worked for George W. Bush, first as director of communications while he was governor of Texas, then as a counselor while he was President of the United States.

Hughes left the Bush administration in July 2002 to return to Texas, but remained in daily contact with the Bush re-election campaign by telephone and email, speaking personally with Bush several times a week. In August 2004, she returned to full-time service with the Bush campaign, planning the 2004 Republican National Convention and the late stages of the 2004 election. She has been described by *The Dallas Morning News* as "the most powerful woman ever to serve in the White House," and by ABC News as Bush's "most essential advisor."

The stirring words on her desk sign were originally written by Winston Churchill.

> I WAS NOT THE LION, BUT IT FELL TO ME TO GIVE THE LION'S ROAR.

ALI KASIKCI

Named the Independent Hotelier of the World in 2004, Ali Kasikci is considered to be one of the hospitality industry's foremost pioneers.

A 20-year veteran of the industry, Mr. Kasikci completed his apprenticeship in Hotel Bayerischer Hof in Munich, Germany and held senior management positions with leading hotels in Germany and with casino resorts in South Africa. His U.S. experience includes five years with Four Seasons Hotels and Resorts in Newport Beach, California prior to joining The Peninsula Beverly Hills in 1992. For nearly 16 years, he was Managing Director of The Peninsula Beverly Hills, the only Mobil Five Star and AAA Five Diamond hotel in Southern California and a member of the prestigious Peninsula Group collection of hotels.

In line with the distinguished reputation of the hotel, Mr. Kasikci was selected as one of the top three hoteliers in the world by *Gourmet Magazine.*

> COMFORT IS A GIVEN AT A GOOD HOTEL.
> IT'S THE ABSENCE OF DISCOMFORT,
> THE DETAILS,
> THAT MAKE A HOTEL GREAT.

JOHN WAYNE

Born Marion Robert Morrison in Winterset, Iowa, John Wayne epitomized rugged masculinity and has become an enduring American icon.

He is famous for his distinctive voice, walk and height. In 2006 *Premiere Magazine* ran an industry poll in which Wayne's portrayal of Ethan Edwards in "The Searchers" was rated the 87th greatest performance in film history. He took part in creating the Motion Picture Alliance for the Preservation of American Ideals in 1943 and was elected president of that organization in 1947. He was an ardent anti-communist, and vocal supporter of the House Un-American Activities Committee.

John Wayne's enduring status as an iconic American was formally recognized by the United States Congress on May 26, 1979 when he was awarded the Congressional Gold Medal.

THERE'S NO LIMIT TO WHAT A MAN CAN DO, OR WHERE HE CAN GO, SO LONG AS HE DOESN'T CARE WHO GETS THE CREDIT.

J.C. WATTS

He is an American conservative Republican politician, CNN political contributor, former Representative from Oklahoma in the U.S. Congress, and former quarterback for the University of Oklahoma.

Watts captured national attention in 1996 with a speech before the Republican national convention, when he said, "You see character does count. For too long we have gotten by in a society that says the only thing right is to get by and the only thing wrong is to get caught. Character is doing what's right when nobody is looking."

Chairman of the J.C. Watts Companies, he works with clients on strategies for business development, communications and public affairs, currently attempting to develop a television news channel that emphasizes news provision from an African American perspective.

Pray

Cornelius C. Pitts

He came to Washington from New Orleans during World War II. At first, he worked as a clerk-typist for the War Department and moonlighted as a cab driver, saving his money for something bigger.

In 1950 Pitts made the leap, buying his first building on Belmont Street, then a middle-class black residential neighborhood. Nine years later he bought another building on Belmont. He went to college, and in 1964, at the age of 41, he graduated with a degree in business administration from Howard University. The next year he bought three more buildings on Belmont Street, then tore down all his buildings and constructed the Pitts Motor Hotel.

In the sixties, the Pitts Hotel was a showplace, and Cornelius Pitts was one of Washington's most successful black entrepreneurs.

THE TROUBLE WITH SOME PEOPLE IS THAT THEY WON'T ADMIT THEIR FAULTS. I'D ADMIT MINE ...IF I HAD ANY.

CLARENCE THOMAS

He has served as an Associate Justice of the Supreme Court of the United States since 1991, the second African American to serve on the nation's highest court (after Thurgood Marshall).

As director of EEOC, he supervised federal efforts to curb discrimination in the workplace. He dramatically changed the practice of the EEOC under his leadership, abandoning the use of timetables and numeric goals, which allowed companies more flexibility in their hiring of minorities. Appointed by President George H. W. Bush, Thomas's career in the Supreme Court has seen him take a conservative approach to cases while adhering to the principle of originalism.

He has been referred to as the leading conservative in America.

DO NOT EMANATE INTO THE PENUMBRA.

WERNHER VON BRAUN

He is considered the preeminent rocket engineer of the 20th century. He worked on the American intercontinental ballistic missile (ICBM) program before joining NASA, where he served as director of NASA's Marshall Space Flight Center and the chief architect of the Saturn V launch vehicle, the superbooster that propelled the Apollo spacecraft to the Moon.

He is generally regarded as the father of the United States space program, both for his technical and organizational skills, and for his public relations efforts on behalf of space flight. He received the 1975 National Medal of Science.

After leaving NASA, von Braun became Vice President for Engineering and Development at the aerospace company, Fairchild Industries.

LATE TO BED. EARLY TO RISE.
WORK LIKE HELL,
AND ADVERTISE.

MORTIMER B. ZUCKERMAN

He is a magazine editor, publisher, and real estate billionaire, regularly named as one of America's wealthiest people.

He is publisher/owner of the *New York Daily News* and Editor-in-Chief of *U.S. News & World Report.* He co-founded Boston Properties, Inc. with substantial real-estate holdings in Boston, New York, Washington, and San Francisco.

In addition to his publishing and real-estate interests, Zuckerman is also a frequent commentator on world affairs, both as an editorialist and on television. He occasionally appears on *The McLaughlin Group* and writes columns for *U.S. News & World Report* and the *New York Daily News*, usually taking positions consistent with American conservatism on political matters.

THE MISHEGOSS STOPS HERE.

KEN BLANCHARD

He is a management expert and author of *The One Minute Manager* (co-authored with Spencer Johnson), a book that has sold over 13 million copies and has been translated into 37 languages. Blanchard is the "chief spiritual officer" of The Ken Blanchard Companies, an international management training and consulting firm that he and his wife, Marjorie Blanchard, co-founded in 1979 in San Diego, California.

Among many accolades, Blanchard has been honored as one of the top 10 Leadership professionals in the international Leadership Gurus survey for 2007 and 2008. The "Leadership Gurus survey" award, by Global Gurus International identifies the top and most influential Leadership professionals in the world by merit and public voting.

Blanchard is a visiting professor at the Cornell University School of Hotel Administration.

> PEOPLE WHO PRODUCE GOOD RESULTS FEEL GOOD ABOUT THEMSELVES.

BILLY GRAHAM

Evangelist Billy Graham has been a spiritual adviser to multiple U.S. presidents and was number seven on Gallup's list of admired people for the 20th century.

Graham has preached in person to more people around the world than any Protestant who has ever lived. It is said that more than 2.5 million people had stepped forward at his crusades to accept Jesus Christ as their personal savior. His lifetime audience, including radio and television broadcasts, has topped two billion.

He has said that his desk sign is there to remind him to keep his messages simple so even the most uneducated person could understand the teachings of the gospel message.

KEEP IT SIMPLE, STUPID.

JOHN C. STENNIS

He was a Democratic U.S. Senator from the state of Mississippi who served for over 41 years, becoming its most senior member by his retirement.

Stennis was unanimously selected President pro tempore of the Senate during the 100th Congress. During his Senate career he chaired, at various times, the Select Committee on Standards and Conduct, the Armed Services Committee, and the Appropriations Committee.

Because of his work with the Armed Services Committee he became known as the "Father of America's Modern Navy," and he was subsequently honored by having a supercarrier named after him. He is one of only two members of Congress to be so honored.

LOOK AHEAD.

SAM ERVIN

Democratic U.S. Senator from North Carolina from 1954 until 1974, Ervin was a self-described "old country lawyer" who became a national figure during the investigation of the Watergate scandals. As chairman of the Senate Select Committee to Investigate Campaign Practices which was established to investigate Watergate, Ervin was a major figure in Nixon's downfall.

With his arching eyebrows and flapping jowls that signaled his moral indignation at much of the testimony before his committee, his half-country, half-courtly demeanor and his predilection for making points by quoting the Bible and Shakespeare and telling folksy stories, Ervin became a hero to many.

> NO MAN'S LIFE, LIBERTY OR PROPERTY IS SAFE WHILE THE LEGISLATURE IS IN SESSION.

GEORGE ALLEN

NFL coach George Allen was considered one of the hardest working coaches in football. He is credited by some with popularizing the coaching trend of 16-hour (or longer) work-days. He sometimes slept at the Redskin Park complex he designed.

Allen was known for his tendency to prefer veteran players to rookies and younger players. During his early years with Washington, the team was known as the "Over the Hill Gang," due to the number of players on the team with lots of past NFL experience. The phrase "the future is now" is often associated with Allen.

Coach Allen would later be appointed by President Ronald Reagan to the President's Council on Physical Fitness and Sports.

> **IF NOT US, WHO?**
> **IF NOT NOW, WHEN?**

Ron Paul

Republican United States Congressman, physician, bestselling author, and two-time presidential candidate, Ron Paul has an active base of supporters that has been coined the "Ron Paul Revolution." He has been described as conservative, Constitutionalist, and libertarian. He favors withdrawal from the North Atlantic Treaty Organization and the United Nations, citing the dangers of foreign entanglements to national sovereignty.

Having pledged never to raise taxes, he has long advocated ending the federal income tax, scaling back government spending, abolishing most federal agencies, and removing military bases and troops from foreign soil; he favors hard money and opposes the Federal Reserve.

Don't steal.
The Government hates competition.

THOMAS S. NEUBERGER

Civil Rights attorney Thomas S. Neuberger, born and raised in Wilmington, Delaware, founded a public accounting firm in May of 1981 after practicing as a partner in a medium sized Wilmington law firm.

As a result of his expertise in the First and Fourteenth Amendments to the Constitution, he was twice honored by being asked to testify before committees of the U.S. Congress. Besides his experience representing clients in civil trials and appeals, he has lectured other lawyers and students on areas of federal court practice and procedure, litigation tactics, the First Amendment of the U.S. Constitution and recent case developments.

The words on his desk are from Matthew 12:26.

WITH GOD ALL THINGS ARE POSSIBLE.

Hilary Hinton "Zig" Ziglar

He is a popular American motivational speaker and self-help author. He came from humble beginnings to be an expert salesman, best-selling author, and highly sought after public speaker.

Ziglar has successfully blended his own religious beliefs with positive thinking to create a philosophy that is his own. Over his long and successful career he has published more than twenty-five books on leadership, personal growth, sales, faith, family, Christianity, and success. He has also published and recorded a long list of audio programs, videos, books and training curriculums for individuals, small businesses, Fortune 500 companies, churches, and nonprofit organizations.

The words on his desk are from Romans 8: 28.

> And we know that in all things God works for the good of those who love him, who have been called according to his purpose.

JOHN GHEGAN

He served as president and CEO of Professional Insurance Company; president of Pennsylvania Life Insurance Company; senior vice president of marketing for Pennsylvania Life Insurance Company; vice-president of sales for Mutual of Omaha for their Northeast and Southeast regions; vice-president of marketing and sales for St. Paul Life Insurance Company and Western Life Insurance Company.

After leaving the Financial Services Industry in 1997, Ghegan used his extensive business experience as an entrepreneur and business owner to consultant several emerging, small, and mid-size businesses.

> IF I HAD IT TO DO
> ALL OVER AGAIN,
> I'D GET HELP.

EDWARD L. KIMBALL

He was the twelfth president of The Church of Jesus Christ of Latter-day Saints from 1973 until his death. He had a vision of a greatly expanded ministry and urged church members to pray for more nations to be opened to the preaching of the gospel.

He constantly counseled church members to "lengthen their stride," as he increased the number of missionaries and accelerated Temple building at a pace never before seen in the church. Despite Kimball's age and history of poor health, major developments occurred during his presidency.

Notable is the 1978 declaration conferring the priesthood on all worthy male members. Prior to this declaration, black males of African descent were not permitted to obtain the priesthood.

Do It.

Robert A. Young III

He joined the Arkansas Best Corporation, a diversified transportation holding company headquartered in Fort Smith, Arkansas, as the Supervisor of Terminal Operations.

Young subsequently held positions as President of DataTronics, Arkansas Best's management information systems subsidiary, then Vice-President of Finance. He became president of the company in 1973. In July 2004, Young added the title of Chairman of the Board of Arkansas Best Corporation to his duties for the Company. In addition to his work at the Company, he has been actively involved in numerous industry and civic organizations.

He currently serves in leadership roles at the American Trucking Associations and the Arkansas Trucking Association as well as serving on the Board of Directors of the Little Rock, AR Branch of the Federal Reserve Bank of St. Louis.

NO SURPRISES

DICK VAN DYKE

Actor Dick Van Dyke starred in a popular situation comedy called *The Dick Van Dyke Show*, from 1961 to 1966 in which he played a comedy writer named Rob Petrie.

He won three Emmy Awards and the series received four Emmy Awards as outstanding comedy series. From 1993 to 2001 Van Dyke portrayed Dr. Mark Sloan in the long running television series *Diagnosis Murder*, a medical/crime drama.

He was a great admirer of Stan Laurel and even gave the eulogy at his funeral. He also produced a TV special, *A Salute to Stan Laurel*. He once met Laurel and told him he had copied a great deal from him. He said Laurel only laughed and said, "I've noticed that."

When everyone desires to be #1, his desk sign suggests a more humble ambition.

I AM THIRD.

JOHN MAXWELL

He is an author, speaker and "leadership expert." He followed his father into the ministry, completing a bachelor's degree at Ohio Christian University in 1969, a Master of Divinity degree at Azusa Pacific University, and a Doctor of Ministry degree at Fuller Theological Seminary.

Every year he speaks to Fortune 500 companies, international government leaders, and organizations as diverse as the US Military Academy at West Point and the National Football League.

As a best-selling author, Maxwell was one of 25 authors and artists named to Amazon.com's 10th Anniversary Hall of Fame. Three of his books, *The 21 Irrefutable Laws of Leadership*, *Developing the Leader Within You*, and *The 21 Indispensable Qualities of a Leader* have each sold over a million copies.

YESTERDAY ENDED LAST NIGHT.
TODAY MATTERS.

YOSHIAKI NAKAZAWA

He is the president of Stryker Japan, one of the world's leading manufacturers of surgical implants and instruments.

A graduate in business from Keio University and Western Michigan University, Nakazawa had a stint at Pfizer before coming back to head up Stryker Japan in 1999. The biggest demand in Japan is for orthopedic hip and knee replacement products, says Nakazawa, adding that the most exciting developments are occurring in the field of biotechnology with the aim of finding bone protein to regenerate joints. Under his leadership, Stryker Japan has captured more than 30% of the Japanese market.

His company's Japanese brochure is full of inspirational movie scenes from *Rocky, Apollo 13* and *Die Hard.*

ACTION

JON M. HUNTSMAN

A self-made billionaire, businessman and philanthropist, Jon M. Huntsman is the founder of Huntsman Corporation and a member of the Forbes 400.

He grew up in humble circumstances, graduated from the Wharton School, worked as a staff member in the Nixon administration, and finally worked for Dow Chemical Company before starting his own business in 1982. That business grew into a multi-billion dollar company, Huntsman Chemical.

At one time, Huntsman made a $54 million deal to sell a portion of his business on a handshake. By the time the deal was completed, the value of the business had increased to $225 million. The CEO he was dealing with offered to split the difference, but Huntsman kept to the original agreed upon deal.

> THE GREATEST EXERCISE FOR THE HUMAN HEART IS TO REACH DOWN AND LIFT ANOTHER UP.

BARRY BERACHA

Chairman of the Board of Pepsi Bottling Group, Beracha previously served as an Executive Vice President of Sara Lee Corporation and Chief Executive Officer of Sara Lee Bakery Group.

He was the Chairman of the Board and Chief Executive Officer of the Earthgrains Company from 1993 to August 2001. Earthgrains was formerly part of Anheuser-Busch Companies, where Mr. Beracha served from 1967 to 1996. From 1979 to 1993, he held the position of Chairman of the Board of Anheuser-Busch Recycling Corporation. From 1976 to 1995, Mr. Beracha was also Chairman of the Board of Metal Container Corporation.

Beracha is also a director of Hertz Global Holdings, Inc. and Chairman of the Board of Trustees of St. Louis University.

> IN GOD WE TRUST.
> ALL OTHERS
> BRING DATA.

JAMES PARKER

He is the former CEO of Southwest Airlines, well-known for its innovative marketing, passenger service and airport selection strategies.

While other airlines announced they were cutting their workforces at least 20 percent in the wake of the post-9/11 drop in business, Southwest kept all its employees on its payroll, and even went ahead with a $179.8 million profit-sharing payment to employees three days after the attacks. Southwest didn't ground its airplanes, while other carriers cut their capacity sharply. Parker's conservative financial strategy had left it with a lot of money in the bank and relatively little debt.

Thirty years of doing things the right way had given the company the strength to do the right things during the worst crisis in the history of aviation.

NO WHINING

MICHAEL D. NIZIOLEK

He was Vice President Human Resources at Hasbro Games, working for the company for 39 years. He believed that when it comes to adding staff, your mantra needs to be "get the best." Avoid hiring just anybody. Better people will make a business more successful. And while better people are usually going to cost more, they will make a difference.

Niziolek served on the Board of Trustees of Springfield Technical Community College, the Regional Employment Board, the Commonwealth Corporation, the Western Massachusetts Chapter of National Conference for Community and Justice, the Economical Development Council of Western Mass., City Stage, and the Spirit of Springfield.

He was also a sports enthusiast, an avid golfer, and former triathlete, qualifying for and competing in the 1993 Hawaii Ironman.

WHY?

SIDNEY HARMAN

He began his audio career in 1953 when he and partner Bernard Kardon developed the world's first stereo receiver. Harman bought out his partner in 1956 and then expanded Harman Kardon into an audio powerhouse, producing high-end home-audio gear under names like Harmon/Kardon, JBL, UREI, Soundcraft, Allen & Heath, Studer, DOD, Lexicon, AKG, BSS, Orban, DBX, Quested and Turbosound.

Under his leadership the company also became a powerhouse in OEM sound systems and electronics sold to automakers. In the 1970s, Harman was appointed undersecretary of the Department of Commerce during the Carter administration.

His wife is U.S. Representative Jane Harmon, Democrat of California.

> IN EVERY BUSINESS THERE IS ALWAYS SOMEONE WHO KNOWS EXACTLY WHAT IS GOING ON. THAT PERSON SHOULD BE FIRED.

SAM MERCANTI

President of Carstar Automotive Canada, a collision repair franchise, Mercanti has grown the company from seven Hamilton-locations in 1994 to 112 in 10 Canadian provinces, with a projected 200 locations within five years.

He has market development managers scouting out locations in every province, looking for potential sites for start-ups for existing independent shops with good operators and strong reputations. His franchisees regularly increase annual sales by 50 to 100 per cent.

Twice nominated for Entrepreneur of the Year and a two-time Hamilton Chamber of Commerce award winner, Mercanti religiously keeps on top of the numbers contained in monthly reports to head office and insurance companies.

WHAT GETS MEASURED, GETS DONE.

HERMAN MELVILLE

An American novelist, short story writer, essayist and poet, Melville was born into a large, well-respected, literary family in New York in 1819.

He attempted to support his family by working various jobs, from banking to teaching school, however, it was his adventures as a seaman in 1845 that inspired Melville to write. In 1851, he completed his masterpiece, *Moby-Dick, or the Whale*. Considered by modern scholars to be one of the great American novels, the book was dismissed by Melville's contemporaries and he made little money from the effort.

It wasn't until the 1920s that the literary public began to recognize Melville as one of America's greatest writers.

Keep True to the Dreams of Thy Youth.

JAMES O'TOOLE

Management guru James O'Toole is Research Professor in the Center for Effective Organizations at the University of Southern California.

He has served as Special Assistant to the Secretary of Health, Education, and Welfare, as Chairman of the Secretary's Task Force on Work in America, and as Director of the USC Twenty-Year Forecast Project (1974-1983) where he interpreted social, political, and economic change for the top management of 30 of the largest US corporations. O'Toole's research and writings are in the areas of leadership, ethics, corporate culture, and philosophy. He is the author of more than 70 journal articles and book chapters that stem from his research.

He also is the author of 14 books, including *Vanguard Management*, named by Business Week as one of the best business and economics books of 1985.

DON'T TRUST ANY WISDOM
OR ADVICE THAT CAN BE
DISTILLED DOWN TO FIT IN
THIS LITTLE SPACE.

KURT MEYER

A practicing Marriage and Family Counselor for over 30 years, Kurt Meyer received his Masters Degree from Roosevelt University in 1955. He studied under the renowned Educational Psychologist, Dr. George W. Hartmann and interned under Dr. Carrero at the Chicago State Hospital where he worked with female alcoholics.

He is a founding clinical member of the International Alliance for Family Life, a professional organization for Marriage and Family Counselors and Educators.

Meyer is well known on the lecture circuits and it was his lecture on "Why We Should Do Away with Marriage Counselors." Though the lecture was done tongue in cheek, it pointed out that most marriage counselors are never called into the act until the marriage has all but perished.

> THE ONLY WAY AROUND
> A PROBLEM IS THROUGH IT.

DONALD J. HALL

He is Chairman of the Board and majority shareholder of Hallmark Cards, the world's largest greeting card manufacturer and one of the world's largest privately held companies.

He was one of three children of Joyce Hall who started selling greeting cards out of Kansas City YMCAs at the age of fifteen and subsequently founded Hallmark Cards, which quickly grew into a major corporation. During Hall's tenure as head of Hallmark, he expanded the company into both crayons (buying Crayola products) and television production (Hallmark Entertainment). Hallmark's greeting card operation also began consistently to account for more than half of all greeting cards sold in the United States.

He is one of Kansas City's billionaires, and the Hall Family Foundation, which he founded, is one of the largest philanthropic organizations in the United States.

The Enemy of Better is Best.

C. MICHAEL ARMSTRONG

He is the former AT&T chairman and CEO, who tried to reestablish AT&T as an end-to-end carrier.

With the dot-com collapse, fraud-assisted telecom depression, unyielding regulatory battles, high debt load, and the sheer complexity and size of the acquisitions, Armstrong was forced to break AT&T up in 2001. He had joined AT&T in 1997 after five and a half years as chairman and CEO of the Hughes Electronics subsidiary of General Motors Corporation. At Hughes, he expedited development of DirecTV to establish one of the first digital-broadcast systems.

Armstrong had joined Hughes after 31 years with **IBM** Corporation, where he eventually led international operations and was a member of **IBM**'s senior executive committee.

ASSUME NOTHING.

Paul F. Harron

Cable television pioneer Paul F. Harron, Jr. cultivated and expanded the cable and broadcasting business of his late father, Paul F. Harron, Sr.

Under his leadership, Harron Communications became one of the largest cable television companies in the nation. He invested in television, radio, independent films, and venture capitalism during his career. He started a cable advertising firm, Metrobase Cable Advertising, which was later sold to Comcast Corp. He was also a founding board member of C-Span. In 1999, Harron sold his company's cable subscribers to Adelphia Communications Corp. in a deal that was the most-noted of his 35-year career.

Outside of communications, Harron owned the Vesper Club, a Philadelphia eating club, racehorses, and a sailboat named the "Miss Conduct."

No Guts, No Glory

JOHN O'CONNOR

A long-time environmental activist, O'Connor is best known as the leader of the National Toxics Campaign, a ground breaking effort he founded in 1983 to raise consciousness about the deadly impact of abuses perpetuated by unregulated chemical companies.

The campaign, at its height, was a major national force for change. O'Connor later became the chairman of Gravestar Inc., an assets management company with a mission to stay committed to the environment and the community. In 1991, he also founded Greenworks, a company that incubates environmental start-up companies.

A candidate for Congress in 1998, *The Boston Globe* described him as a "tough competitor but warm and generous with a zeal for life."

The Fun is in the Fight.

CHARLES E. WILSON

He received an engineering degree in 1909 at Carnegie Tech University. A distinguished career in industry led to Wilson's appointment as vice president of General Motors in 1928 and president by 1941.

During World War II, he directed the company's huge defense production effort, which earned him a U.S. Medal of Merit in 1946. In 1944, as the director of the War Production Board, he told the Army Ordnance Board that in order to prevent a return to the Great Depression, the United States needed "a permanent war economy." This permanent war economy would evolve into the modern military-industrial complex. During World War II, Wilson directed GM's outstanding performance in producing tanks, aircraft engines, trucks, and munitions.

In 1953, President Dwight D. Eisenhower selected Wilson as his Secretary of Defense.

> WHAT'S GOOD FOR GENERAL MOTORS IS GOOD FOR AMERICA AND WHAT'S GOOD FOR AMERICA IS GOOD FOR GENERAL MOTORS.

DAVID MILIBAND

He is the current Secretary of State for Foreign and Commonwealth Affairs and Member of British Parliament.

Miliband is a graduate of Corpus Christi College, Oxford, where he achieved first class honours in Philosophy, Politics and Economics. From 1988 to 1989 he took an S.M. degree in Political Science at MIT, where he was a Kennedy Scholar. Miliband is a social democrat and seen as Blairite in terms of advocating choice in public services. He is generally believed to be on the left of the New Labour project, advocating better action on the environment, higher public spending and a more Pro-European foreign policy.

Miliband is the current favorite to succeed Gordon Brown as leader of the Labour Party.

Positive Thinking Zone

W. Clement Stone

He began his working career by selling of newspapers in restaurants and corner diners. At the time, this deviated from the normal practice of young boys hawking newspapers on street corners. At first, the managers of the eateries tried to discourage him from this practice, but he gradually won them over, due in part to his politeness, charm, persistence and the fact that, by and large, the patrons had no objection to this new way of getting their daily paper.

In 1919, Stone built the Combined Insurance Company of America, and, by 1930, he had over 1000 agents selling insurance for him across the United States. By 1979, Stone's insurance company exceeded $1 billion in assets.

Stone always emphasized using a "positive mental attitude" to make money.

Do It Now.

JOEL HYATT

He is the founder of Hyatt Legal Services, and was featured in the law firm's television commercials announcing, "I'm Joel Hyatt and you have my word on it."

Hyatt graduated from Dartmouth College and Yale Law School, then briefly practiced law as an associate at Paul, Weiss, Rifkind, Wharton & Garrison. Hyatt co-founded Hyatt Legal Services in 1977 as a low-cost legal service and later founded Hyatt Legal Plans, which became the country's largest provider of employer-sponsored group legal services. He was a founding member of the U.S. Senate Democratic Leadership Circle and was a member of that group from 1981 to 1986. He was the Democratic National Committee's assistant treasurer from 1981 to 1983.

The words on his desk sign originated with Carthaginian General Hannibal.

> WE WILL EITHER FIND A WAY OR WE WILL MAKE ONE.

HARVEY A. GOLDSTEIN

He is a Certified Public Accountant and Chairman of the Southern California CPA firm of Singer, Lewak, Greenbaum & Goldstein.

During the course of his 35 years of professional service, Goldstein has attained a wide level of experience with clients in a variety of industries including manufacturing, wholesale/distribution, law firms, printing, and professional services. He has consulted with clients on mergers and acquisitions, financing, strategic planning, software development, profit enhancement, cash flow management, marketing, and a variety of corporate management issues.

He is the author of *Up Your Cash Flow*, cited by *USA Today* as one of the 10 business books that "should be on every business owner's book shelf."

> GOOD THINGS COME TO
> THOSE WHO WAIT —
> BUT ONLY THOSE THINGS LEFT
> BY THOSE WHO HUSTLE.

OPRAH WINFREY

Born in rural Mississippi to a poor teenage single mother and later raised in an inner city Milwaukee neighborhood, Oprah Winfrey became a television host, media mogul, and philanthropist.

Her internationally-syndicated talk show, *The Oprah Winfrey Show*, has earned her multiple Emmy Awards and is the highest-rated talk show in the history of television. Credited with creating a more intimate confessional form of media communication, she is thought to have popularized and revolutionized the tabloid talk show genre. She is also an influential book critic, an Academy Award nominated actress, and a magazine publisher. She has been ranked the richest African American of the 20th century, the most philanthropic African American of all time.

She is also, according to some assessments, the most influential woman in the world.

SURROUND YOURSELF WITH ONLY PEOPLE WHO ARE GOING TO LIFT YOU HIGHER.

JOHN C. SAWHILL

He was president and CEO of The Nature Conservancy and the 12th President of New York University (NYU).

Sawhill earned a PhD in economics in 1963 from New York University, where he served as professor of economics. He was named president of New York University in 1975, serving until 1979. At a trying time in NYU's history, he received widespread acclaim for bringing about an academic and financial turnaround at the country's largest private university. His research focused on the nonprofit sector, and his seminar "Effective Leadership of Social Enterprises" prepared students for leadership roles in nonprofit management.

During his ten-year tenure, The Nature Conservancy became the world's largest private conservation group and protected more than 7 million acres in the United States alone.

IF YOU'RE NOT THE LEAD DOG,
THE VIEW NEVER CHANGES.

DIRCK HALSTEAD

Photojournalist, and editor and publisher of *The Digital Journalist*, Dirck Halstead became Life magazine's youngest combat photographer covering the Guatemalan Civil War.

After attending Haverford College, he went on to work for UPI for more than 15 years. During the Vietnam War he was UPI's picture bureau chief in Saigon. In 1972 he accepted a contract with *Time* covering the White House for the next 29 years. Halstead was one of six photographers who accompanied Richard Nixon to China in 1972. His photographs have appeared on 47 *Time* covers, more than any other photographer.

Halstead is now spearheading the evolution of photojournalism from a static medium dependent on paper-printed vehicles, into a multi-disciplinary, multi-media hybrid that incorporates the elements of print, radio, and visual journalism.

I AM ONLY INTERESTED IN LONG TERM PERFORMANCE.

Franz Kafka

He was one of the major fiction writers of the 20th century. Kafka's unique body of writing is considered by some people to be among the most influential in Western literature.

The apparent hopelessness and absurdity that seem to permeate his works are considered emblematic of existentialism. Kafka's sentences then deliver an unexpected impact just before the full stop—that being the finalizing meaning and focus. Biographers have said that it was common for Kafka to read chapters of the books he was working on to his closest friends, and that those readings usually concentrated on the humorous side of his prose.

His desk sign reminded him to allow a story to mature in his head before writing it down.

WAIT.

JIMMY HOFFA

Labor leader Jimmy Hoffa served as president of the International Brotherhood of Teamsters from the mid-1950s to the mid-1960s.

He took over the presidency of the Teamsters in 1957, when his predecessor, Dave Beck, was convicted on bribery charges and imprisoned. Hoffa worked to expand the union and in 1964 succeeded in bringing virtually all North American over-the-road truck drivers under a single national master freight agreement. Hoffa then pushed to try to bring the airlines and other transport employees into the union. In 1964, Hoffa was convicted of attempted bribery of a grand juror and jailed for 15 years.

He is also well-known in popular culture for the mysterious circumstances surrounding his unexplained disappearance and presumed death.

ILLEGITIMI NON CARBORUNDUM

(Don't let the bastards wear you down)

DONALD RUMSFELD

He was the 13th Secretary of Defense under President Gerald Ford from 1975 to 1977, and the 21st Secretary of Defense under President George W. Bush from 2001 to 2006.

Rumsfeld was both the youngest (43 years old) and the oldest (74 years old) person to have held the position, as well as the only person to have held the position for two non-consecutive terms, and the second longest serving, behind Robert McNamara. He was White House Chief of Staff during part of the Ford Administration, and also served in various positions in the Nixon Administration. In an unprecedented move in modern US history, eight retired generals and admirals called for Rumsfeld to resign in early 2006 in what was called the "Generals Revolt," accusing him of "abysmal" military planning and lack of strategic competence.

The words on his desk originated with Teddy Roosevelt.

> AGGRESSIVE FIGHTING FOR THE RIGHT IS THE NOBLEST SPORT THE WORLD AFFORDS.

COLIN POWELL

American statesman and a retired four-star general in the United States Army, Colin Powell was the 65th United States Secretary of State, serving under President George W. Bush, the first African American appointed to that position.

During his military career, he also served as National Security Advisor, as Commander-in-Chief, U.S. Army Forces Command and as Chairman of the Joint Chiefs of Staff, holding the latter position during the Gulf War. He was the first, and so far the only, African American to serve on the Joint Chiefs of Staff. A moderate Republican, he is well known for his willingness to support liberal or centrist causes, and in the presidential election of 2008, he announced his endorsement of Barack Obama.

Powell displayed a quotation from Thomas Jefferson on his desk throughout his tenure as chairman of the Joint Chiefs of Staff.

I SHALL OFTEN GO WRONG THROUGH DEFECT OF JUDGMENT. WHEN RIGHT, I SHALL OFTEN BE THOUGHT WRONG BY THOSE WHOSE POSITIONS WILL NOT COMMAND A VIEW OF THE WHOLE GROUND. I ASK YOUR INDULGENCE FOR MY OWN ERRORS, WHICH WILL NEVER BE INTENTIONAL, AND YOUR SUPPORT AGAINST THE ERRORS OF OTHERS, WHO MAY CONDEMN WHAT THEY WOULD NOT IF SEEN IN ALL ITS PARTS.

CURTIS EMERSON LEMAY

The general is credited with designing and implementing an effective systematic strategic bombing campaign in the Pacific Theatre of World War II.

After the war, LeMay headed the Berlin airlift, then reorganized the Strategic Air Command (SAC) into an effective means of conducting nuclear war. He was appointed Vice Chief of Staff of the United States Air Force in July 1957, serving until 1961 when he was made the fifth Chief of Staff of the United States Air Force. His belief in the efficacy of strategic air campaigns over tactical strikes and ground support operations became Air Force policy during his tenure as Chief of Staff.

LeMay became the vice presidential running mate of American Independent Party candidate George Wallace in 1968.

To Err is Human;
to Forgive, Divine.

ALLEN KLEIN

He is a businessman and record label executive. His career highlights include celebrated clients such as the Beatles and the Rolling Stones.

In 1965, Klein replaced Andrew Loog Oldham as business manager of The Rolling Stones. Mick Jagger had studied at the London School of Economics and was impressed enough with Klein's business skills. In 1969, Klein re-negotiated the Beatles contract with EMI, granting them the highest royalties ever paid to an artist at that time. Klein helped John Lennon and Yoko Ono with their film *Imagine*, and helped Harrison to organize the Concert for Bangladesh. He bought the rights to music produced by Phil Spector, such as the Philles Records and Phil Spector International catalogues.

Klein regarded himself as a shrewd and tenacious businessman, exampled by the modified bible quote he kept on his desk.

THOUGH I WALK IN THE SHADOW OF THE VALLEY OF EVIL, I HAVE NO FEAR, AS I AM THE BIGGEST BASTARD IN THE VALLEY.

STANLEY KRAMER

Academy Award-nominated American film director and producer, Stanley Kramer was responsible for some of Hollywood's most famous "message" movies, including *The Defiant Ones, On the Beach, Inherit the Wind, Judgment at Nuremberg*, and *Guess Who's Coming to Dinner*.

After gaining experience in various of the trades associated with filmmaking, he began writing scripts for movies and radio programs in the late 1930s. His first production experience was with the films *So Ends Our Night* and *The Moon and Sixpence*. His success as an independent producer with such films as *So This Is New York, Champion, Home of the Brave*, and *The Men* established him as a major figure in Hollywood. Kramer has the claim to fame of bringing Marlon Brando to the screen for the first time.

The words on his desk refer to Hollywood's inflated egos.

> PLEASE GOD,
> MAKE THE PICTURES BIG
> AND THE HEADS SMALL.

Billy Wilder

He was a journalist, film director, screenwriter, and producer, whose career spanned more than 50 years and 60 films.

Wilder is regarded as one of the most brilliant and versatile filmmakers of Hollywood's golden age. Wilder's first significant success was Ninotchka, a collaboration with fellow German immigrant Ernst Lubitsch. (The urbane comedies of manners gave Lubitsch the reputation of being Hollywood's most elegant and sophisticated director and his films were promoted as having "the Lubitsch touch"). Wilder is responsible for two of the film noir era's most definitive films in *Double Indemnity* and *Sunset Boulevard*.

Along with Woody Allen, he leads the list of films on the American Film Institute's list of 100 funniest American films and holds the honor of holding the top spot with *Some Like it Hot*.

WHAT WOULD LUBITSCH DO?

NEIL MCELROY

He was the president of Procter & Gamble who became Secretary of Defense from 1957 to 1959 under President Eisenhower.

McElroy grew up in Cincinnati, Ohio. After receiving a bachelor's degree in economics from Harvard in 1925, he returned to Cincinnati to work in the advertising department of the Procter & Gamble Company. He advanced rapidly up the managerial ladder and became company president in 1948. Although a well known businessman, McElroy's only experience in the federal government prior to 1957 had been as chairman of the White House Conference on Education in 1955-56.

Given his background in industry, and given President Eisenhower's predominance in defense matters, McElroy's appointment was not unusual.

> **STATE YOUR CASE BEFORE YOU EXPLAIN IT.**

ROBERTO GOIZUETA

He was Chairman, Director, and CEO of the Coca-Cola Company from August 1980 until his death in October 1997.

Under his direction, investors saw the Coca-Cola Company become a top U.S. corporation. Goizueta is credited with invigorating the company with a global vision, and during his tenure, the Coca-Cola brand became the most well-known trademark in the world.

He introduced the Coke slogans: "Coke is It!," "You Can't Beat the Feeling," and "Always Coca-Cola." He launched Diet Coke. In the process, Goizueta created more wealth for shareholders than any other CEO in history.

PLAN IS A FOUR LETTER WORD.

RAY KROC

In 1954, a fifty-two-year-old milk-shake machine salesman by the name of Ray Kroc saw a hamburger stand in San Bernardino, California, and envisioned a massive new industry: fast food.

In what should have been his golden years, the founder and builder of McDonald's Corporation, proved himself an industrial pioneer no less capable than Henry Ford. He revolutionized the American restaurant industry by imposing discipline on the production of hamburgers, french fries, and milk shakes. By developing a sophisticated operating and delivery system, he insured that the french fries customers bought in Topeka would be the same as the ones purchased in New York City. Such consistency made McDonald's the brand name that defined American fast food.

Kroc was included in *Time 100: The Most Important People of the Century.*

> **NOTHING IN THE WORLD CAN TAKE THE PLACE OF PERSISTENCE.**

MIKE KRZYZEWSKI

Head coach of the Duke University men's basketball team, Mike Krzyzewski also coached the United States men's national basketball team at the 2006 world championship and the 2008 Summer Olympics, culminating with the gold medal at the Olympics.

Affectionately known as "Coach K", Krzyzewski has led the Blue Devils to three NCAA Championships, ten Final Fours (third most in history), and ten ACC Championships over 28 seasons at Duke. Currently the winningest active men's coach in the nation, Krzyzewski has amassed an NCAA-record 69 NCAA tournament victories, while averaging more than 25 wins per season.

He has also coached an NCAA record nine 30-win seasons in his tenure. Sixty-one of the 65 four-year players under his tutelage since 1986 have competed in at least one Final Four.

> YOU CAN MODIFY BEHAVIOR BUT YOU CAN'T REHABILITATE CHARACTER.

ROY WILLIAMS

He is the head coach of the men's basketball team at the University of North Carolina. After averaging an 80% win percentage in 15 seasons at the University of Kansas, he became the eighteenth head coach at North Carolina.

It has been concluded through recent polls that Williams is the best college basketball coach to have ever lived. He is second all-time for most wins at Kansas behind Phog Allen, and third all-time in the NCAA for winning percentage. He earned his 400th win in January 2003, when Kansas beat the University of Wyoming. Coach Williams won his 500th career game against High Point University on December 9, 2006 in Chapel Hill. On April 4, 2005, Williams shed his title as "the most successful coach to never have won an NCAA ring" as his Tar Heels defeated the University of Illinois in the 2005 NCAA Championship game.

Williams was inducted into the Basketball Hall of Fame in 2007.

> **STATISTICS ARE IMPORTANT BUT RELATIONSHIPS LAST FOREVER.**

ANDREW WALTER "ANDY" REID

He is the head coach of the Philadelphia Eagles of the NFL. He led the Eagles to four NFC championship game appearances, from 2001-2004 and to Super Bowl XXXIX in 2004.

During his tenure, Reid compiled the best win total (96), winning percentage (.608) and playoff victory total (8) in team history. Since he was hired in 1999, no other franchise has earned more divisional playoff round appearances. Beginning in 2001, Reid's Eagles won the National Football Conference's Eastern Division four consecutive times, the longest such streak in franchise history, and advanced to the conference championship game in 2001, 2002, 2003 and 2004.

The sign on his desk is inscribed with a quotation by Charles Lindbergh.

> THE IMPORTANT THING IS TO LAY A PLAN, THEN FOLLOW IT STEP BY STEP NO MATTER HOW SMALL OR LARGE EACH ONE BY ITSELF MAY SEEM.

ROBERT S. PRATHER

He was the President and Chief Operating Officer of Gray Television, Inc., a television broadcast company.

Prather has served as Chairman of the Board at Triple Crown Media, Inc., a publishing and communication company. He has also served as Chief Executive Officer and director of Bull Run Corporation, a sports and affinity marketing and management company from 1992 until its merger into Triple Crown Media, Inc. Prather is also on the Board of Directors of Nioxin Research Laboratories, Inc., Georgia World Congress Center, Draper Holdings Business Trust, Enterprise Bank, and Swiss Army Brands, Inc.

Prather turned Gray into a "discipline acquirer," buying stations every two or three years then using the time in between the buys to pay down debt.

> EVEN THE MOST EFFICIENT
> DINOSAUR
> IS STILL EXTINCT.

WALTER H. ANNENBERG

Billionaire publisher, philanthropist, and diplomat, Walter H. Annenberg was the son of Moses "Moe" Annenberg, who published *The Daily Racing Form* and *The Philadelphia Inquirer*.

After his father's death, Annenberg took over the family businesses, buying additional print media as well as radio and television stations, resulting in great success. One of his most prominent successes was the creation of *TV Guide* in 1952, which he started against the advice of his financial advisers. Even while an active businessman, Annenberg had an interest in public service. After Richard M. Nixon was elected President, he appointed Annenberg as ambassador to Great Britain.

Over the years, Annenberg became one of the country's biggest philanthropists, giving away more than $2 billion in cash.

> CAUSE MY WORKS ON EARTH TO REFLECT HONOR ON MY FATHER'S MEMORY.

Ralph Waldo Emerson Jones

He served as president of Grambling University for 41 years, dedicated to opening doors through which many poor and disenfranchised students could pass to secure better life quality for themselves and succeeding generations.

Dr. Jones, the grandson of a slave, went to Grambling in 1926, when it was the Lincoln Parish Training School, a two-year teachers' institute. He started out as an instructor in chemistry, physics and mathematics. In his early years there, he started a baseball team, served as dean of men, formed a band and held the post of registrar.

At the age of 30 he became the president of the school and continued to serve as baseball coach while heading the college.

> LOVE YOUR ENEMIES;
> BLESS THEM
> THAT CURSE YOU.

MIKE ROYKO

He was a newspaper columnist in Chicago, Illinois, who won the 1972 Pulitzer Prize for commentary. Over his thirty year career, Royko wrote over 7,500 daily columns for three newspapers, the *Chicago Daily News*, the *Chicago Sun-Times*, and the *Chicago Tribune*.

He grew up in Chicago, living in an apartment above a bar. On becoming a columnist, he drew experiences from his childhood, becoming the voice of the Chicago Everyman. Although caustically sarcastic, he never condescended to his readers, and always remembered he was one of them.

Royko covered Cook County politics and government in a weekly political column, and the success of the column earned him regular writing about all topics for the *Daily News*.

> My job is to comfort the afflicted, and afflict the comfortable.

JOHN MCCAIN

He is the senior United States Senator from Arizona. McCain was the Republican nominee for president in the 2008 United States election.

He retired from the Navy as a captain in 1981, moved to Arizona, and entered politics. Elected to the U.S. House of Representatives in 1982, he served two terms, and was then elected to the U.S. Senate in 1986, winning re-election easily in 1992, 1998, and 2004. While generally adhering to conservative principles, he at times has had a media reputation as a "maverick" for having disagreed with his party. McCain has consistently opposed pork barrel spending by Congress, and he actively supported the Line Item Veto Act of 1996, which gave the president power to veto individual spending items.

The sign on his desk is inscribed with a quotation by Booker T. Washington.

I HAVE LEARNED THAT SUCCESS IS TO BE MEASURED NOT SO MUCH BY THE POSITION THAT ONE HAS REACHED IN LIFE AS BY THE OBSTACLES WHICH HE HAS HAD TO OVERCOME WHILE TRYING TO SUCCEED.

Henry Flagler

Tycoon, real estate promoter, railroad developer and John D. Rockefeller's partner in Standard Oil, Henry Flagler was a key figure in the development of the eastern coast of Florida along the Atlantic Ocean and was founder of what became the Florida East Coast Railway. He is known as the father of Miami, Florida.

It was Flagler's idea to use the rebate system to strengthen Standard Oil's position against competitors and the transporting enterprises alike. Though the refunds issued amounted to no more than fifteen cents, they put the company in position to out-compete other oil refineries. As the company grew through effective business practices, it developed other strongly anti-competitive strategies, including a systematic program of offering to purchase competitors.

Flagler kept a quotation on his desk that summarized the Standard Oil philosophy.

> DO UNTO OTHERS AS THEY WOULD DO UNTO YOU — AND DO IT FIRST.

THOMAS EDISON

One of the most prolific inventors in history, holding 1,093 U.S. patents in his name, Thomas Edison developed many devices that greatly influenced life around the world, including the phonograph and the long-lasting, practical electric light bulb.

Dubbed "The Wizard of Menlo Park" by a newspaper reporter, he is often credited with the creation of the first industrial research laboratory. His advanced work in communication and, in particular, telecommunications, was an outgrowth of his early career as a telegraph operator.

Edison originated the concept and implementation of electric-power generation and distribution to homes, businesses, and factories — a crucial development in the modern industrialized world.

> THERE IS A BETTER WAY
> TO DO IT. FIND IT.

WINSTON CHURCHILL

He served as Prime Minister of the United Kingdom from 1940 to 1945 and again from 1951 to 1955.

A noted statesman and orator, Churchill was also an officer in the British Army, a historian, a Nobel Prize-winning writer, and an artist. Churchill had been among the first to recognize the growing threat of Hitler long before the outset of the Second World War. Although there was an element of British public and political sentiment favoring negotiated peace with a clearly ascendant Germany, Churchill nonetheless refused to consider an armistice with Hitler's Germany. His use of rhetoric hardened public opinion against a peaceful resolution and prepared the British for a long war. Coining the general term for the upcoming battle, Churchill stated in his "finest hour" speech to the House of Commons on June 18, 1940, "I expect that the Battle of Britain is about to begin."

He kept a brass plaque on his desk inscribed with a quotation attributed to Queen Victoria.

> PLEASE UNDERSTAND THERE IS NO DEPRESSION IN THIS HOUSE AND WE ARE NOT INTERESTED IN THE POSSIBILITIES OF DEFEAT. THEY DO NOT EXIST.

HARRY S. TRUMAN

He was the thirty-third President of the United States, succeeding Franklin D. Roosevelt who died less than three months after he began his fourth term.

Truman, whose demeanor was very different from that of the patrician Roosevelt, was a folksy, unassuming president. He overcame the low expectations of many political observers who compared him unfavorably with his highly regarded predecessor. As Senator, Truman had not supported the nascent Civil Rights Movement. As President, however, he integrated the armed forces and appointed the first federal civil rights committee responsible for investigating discrimination based on race or religion.

Many people know about the sign that President Harry Truman had on his desk which read, "The Buck Stops Here," but most don't know the motto he had on his desk while he was a Senator. It was a quotation from fellow Missourian Mark Twain.

> ALWAYS DO RIGHT.
> THIS WILL GRATIFY SOME PEOPLE
> AND ASTONISH THE REST.

INDEX

ALLEN, GEORGE 52
ANNENBERG, WALTER H. 144
ARMSTRONG, C. MICHAEL... 92
BERACHA, BARRY 74
BLANCHARD, KEN 44
BROWNBACK, SAM 24
CHURCHILL, WINSTON 156
EDISON, THOMAS 154
EINSTEIN, ALBERT 4
EISENHOWER, DWIGHT D. 14
ERVIN, SAM 50
FLAGLER, HENRY 152
FORD, HENRY 2
GERSTNER, LOUIS V. 22
GHEGAN, JOHN 60
GIULIANI, RUDOLPH 10
GOIZUETA, ROBERTO 132
GOLDSTEIN, HARVEY A. 106
GRAHAM, BILLY 46
HALL, DONALD J. 90
HALSTEAD, DIRCK 112
HARMAN, SIDNEY 80
HARRON, PAUL F. 94
HOFFA, JIMMY 116
HUGHES, KAREN 28
HUNTSMAN, JON M. 72
HYATT, JOEL 104
JACOBS, JOSEPH J. 20
JONES, RALPH WALDO EMERSON 146

INDEX

KAFKA, FRANZ 114
KASIKCI, ALI 30
KATEN, KAREN 26
KENNEDY, JOHN F. 16
KIMBALL, EDWARD L. 62
KLEIN, ALLEN 124
KRAMER, STANLEY 126
KROC, RAY 134
KRZYZEWSKI, MIKE 136
LEMAY, CURTIS EMERSON 122
MAXWELL, JOHN 68
McCAIN, JOHN 150
McELROY, NEIL 130
MELVILLE, HERMAN 84
MERCANTI, SAM 82
MEYER, KURT 88
MILIBAND, DAVID 100
NAKAZAWA, YOSHIAKI 70
NEUBERGER, THOMAS S. 56
NEWMAN, PAUL 12
NIZIOLEK, MICHAEL D. 78
O'CONNOR, JOHN 96
O'TOOLE, JAMES 86
PARKER, JAMES 76
PAUL, RON 54
PEROT, ROSS 18
PITTS, CORNELIUS C. 36
POWELL, COLIN 120
PRATHER, ROBERT S. 142

INDEX

REAGAN, RONALD 8
REID, ANDREW WALTER "ANDY" 140
ROYKO, MIKE 148
RUMSFELD, DONALD 118
SAWHILL, JOHN C. 110
STENNIS, JOHN C. 48
STONE, W. CLEMENT 102
THOMAS, CLARENCE 38
TRUMAN, HARRY S. 158
TURNER, TED 6
VAN DYKE, DICK 66
VON BRAUN, WERNHER 40
WATTS, J.C. 34
WAYNE, JOHN 32
WILDER, BILLY 128
WILLIAMS, ROY 138
WILSON, CHARLES E. 98
WINFREY, OPRAH 108
YOUNG III, ROBERT A. 64
ZIGLAR, HILARY HINTON "ZIG" 58
ZUCKERMAN, MORTIMER B. 42

www.ingramcontent.com/pod-product-compliance
Lightning Source LLC
Chambersburg PA
CBHW051758040426
42446CB00007B/434